FINANCIAL FREEDOM
A New Beginning

Tony Cash

Author of "Eye Know Why You're Broke; Do You?

ISBN-13: 978-1-7353422-2-1

First printing edition 2022

Ordering Information: Quantity sales. Special discounts are available on quantity purchases by corporations, associations, non-profits and others. For details, contact the author at the address below.

5351 Snapfinger Woods Drive
Decatur, GA 30035

TABLE OF CONTENTS

ACKNOWLEDGMENTS

I have to start by thanking **my awesome wife, Eleshia Cash,** who I affectionately call "**Blue.**" From reminding me daily of my financial knowledge and experience and how the world would benefit from it, to giving me advice on the book subject matter and keeping Kennedy and Jackson out of my hair so I could write. She was as important to this book getting done as I was. Thank you so much, "**Blue.**"

To **Kennedy and Jackson**: Everything I do is to leave a legacy for you. I am so proud of both of you and you inspire me to want to do more, be more and have more in this world.

To my amazing mother, Santina Cash Hines: I so look up to you and you are the most beautiful 70-year-old woman I know. Stay in that gym, Momma. You look great!

I can't forget to say thank you to **Tammy, Dexter and Nic (she swears she's my favorite), & Tamela**; my sisters and brother and for the love each of you have given me over the years.

To **my church family**, "The Leadership Church," I love you.

Finally, to all those who have been a part of my life through friendship, daily calls and relationships, I appreciate you and love you. Special shout out to **Dewayne Kelby (my best friend from the US Navy), Jeanette Pollock, Tim and Vanessa Byrd and Connie Ford**.

I pray that something you read in this book is life changing to your finances and the legacy you leave on the earth.

Tony
Santina's Boy

CHAPTER

1

You Got This!

Over my lifetime, I have learned so much about financial wellbeing and I want to share it with you. I still believe that it is possible for you and me to live a life of financial freedom and I want to encourage you to believe that it's possible.

Whatever your goals are for your personal finances, I want to tell you something...you got this! Wherever you are financially, it is never too bad or too late for your financial life to improve.

As a child from the rough streets of Bankhead Courts in Atlanta, Georgia, I know what it means to struggle financially and have many needs unmet. I know what it means to be stressed due to financial instability and having to trust God for your provisions. I know what it means to have very little and know when it appears like there is no hope! I learned something during that time of my life. I learned that life is hard, but I'm harder. Life is tough, but I'm tougher. Whatever I put my mind to, I can do! I believe that you don't have to struggle financially in life if you choose good financial counsel and use it.

The purpose of this book is to help you understand that financial despair does not have to be your destination. You were not born to be poor; you were born to poor financial conditions. However, the condition you were born into does not have to be the condition that you end with. Throughout this book, I give you hope and belief in yourself to achieve financial freedom. You are empowered to take the steps to be financially free and to have the life you've always dreamed of having. I will say it again: It is possible for you to live with financial freedom...**You Got This!**

You are the Key

One of the things I've noticed about the world today is no one wants to take responsibility for their actions. We live in a world where most things that we don't do right or get right we can trace it back to everything and everybody except ourselves. I believe that this leaves many people feeling less empowered. One of my strongest beliefs in life is that *God has not given us the spirit of fear, but of power, and of love, and of a sound mind.* In my opinion, this is a reminder that we are not to shun personal responsibility for any part of our lives, yet instead be bold about who we are and our purpose in life.

What does it mean for you and me to be bold about our finances? The word "bold" means a willingness to take risks and act innovatively; [to have] confidence or courage. My point is "this is **your** financial life, not the financial life of your family or society. You are the key! You are empowered and you are ultimately responsible for how your financial life turns out. There is beauty in accepting responsibility for the results of your financial life. You get to decide how amazing your financial life will be. You get to decide how much joy you will have in your life and your financial freedom will belong to you and you alone!

> **Being rich is having money; being wealthy is having time.**
>
> *Margaret Bonanno*

Remember what I've said, you are the key. A key opens doors. Even if you have the wrong key for the door you are trying to open, that key still has the power to open a door. The challenge is finding the right door. Stop and think about this for a minute. The value of the key isn't diminished because it did not work in the first door.

I wish there was a financial book that was a "one size fits all," and as a matter of fact I wish I were the author of that book. However, there is no such book. You ultimately decide where you would like to go with your finances. You ultimately decide that you are going to get educated about finances. Everything, especially your financial freedom, rises and fall with your level of desire. If you decide that you are going to be passionate about financial freedom, then you will get there. However, if you decide just living paycheck to paycheck is good enough for you, then happy payday because that is all you will get in this life, a paycheck!

Envision Your Financial Freedom

For some people, trying to envision being financially free can paralyze them. A person thinks *"How can someone like me ever be financially free? I didn't come from a wealthy family, and I've made too many financial mistakes."* This is simply fear speaking negatively against your blessed future. You must confront your fear and the notion that you are not worthy to be financially free. Once you confront your fear, you're empowered to live financially free and experience all the joys that come along with that!

> **Financial freedom is available to those who learn about it and work for it.**
>
> *Robert Kiyosaki*

Financial freedom happens when we decide that we are no longer okay with being broke, busted, and disgusted! I believe that once someone decides that no matter how hard it is and how long it takes, he or she is going to be financially free, it can be done.

As you read this book, remain hopeful about your financial future. As you think positively, God and life will begin to bring positivity to your life. I can't say that becoming financially free will be easy. However, I do believe that if you keep learning, keep seeking and keep applying great financial wisdom such as what you'll find in this book, you will begin to see a great improvement in your financial life. Hopefully this motivates you to keep going and never stop.

I am on this journey with you and my hope is that throughout this journey together, you realize how beautiful life can be when you walk in financial freedom.

My prayer is that if anyone is without financial hope, let it not be for any reason other than choice. I believe everyone deserves financial freedom.

Take ACTION

Be honest with yourself about your financial behavior and habits.

Write down all the financial mistakes you've made.

Vow and commit to not make those mistakes again.

While everything that pertains to your financial status up to this point may not be your fault, it's *your* responsibility from this point forward.

Financial freedom is one of many journeys you will take in life; and just like God helped you through every other journey in your life, he will help you through your financial journey.

Tony

CHAPTER

2

How Did We Lose Our Financial Freedom?

As someone who has helped thousands of people with their finances, I have often heard people in financial exasperation say, *"I don't know how I lost my financial freedom!"* I have always interpreted this statement to mean, *"What happened to my money?"* *"How did I get in so much debt?"* *"What happened to the 18-year-old who said, 'I'm not going to be financially stressed and unprepared like my parents'?"* These statements are spoken by people who are living lives where there is never enough, always needing more and unable to enjoy life.

I believe it all starts with people who do not give the proper attention to their finances. It's similar to anything else in our lives that we do not give the proper attention to, such as health, family, and relationships; if we fail to give it the proper attention, we are basically accepting defeat in that area of our lives.

Life moves faster than we know. First came our friends, significant others, children, jobs, and suddenly, we looked up and found that we had forgotten about the importance of preparing for a healthy financial future. In addition, debt and bills started to slowly become the norm in our lives; and before long we were just used to working to pay the bills. We grew accustomed to living from paycheck to paycheck and now, here we are!

I can't tell you the countless stories I've heard from ordinary people about how life just seemed to creep up on them and before they knew it, they were financially overwhelmed.

I love the bible quote that says, *"Too much sleep and folding of the hands and want shall come upon thee, as a traveler, and poverty as a man armed. But if thou be diligent, thy harvest shall come as a fountain, and want shall flee."* The truth is that we are responsible for our financial freedom. When it's all said and done, there is no one else who is responsible for our financial success.

Be Financially Responsible

God gives each of us the gift of time and money. Now, maybe he doesn't give them to us in equal portions, but he does give them to us. We bear the responsibility of being good stewards of both. We bear the responsibility of ensuring that the gifts of time and money are not wasted but treasured.

My wife, Eleshia and I have made great sacrifices to have a financially free life. I can tell you that it wasn't easy coming together, as we were from vastly different childhood experiences and backgrounds. It's fair to say that we had our struggles in the beginning. However, once we realized that no one was going to come into our home and force us to be financially responsible, we accepted responsibility for our financial lives.

What I'm saying is that you need to accept the responsibility and be accountable for your finances. The only person who can ensure that you are financially successful is you and I believe with a little hard work and personal dedication, you can do it.

I can honestly say that every financial test and trial that my wife and I went through caused me to look deeper at myself and the financial decisions I made. Then I told myself that *"I have to do better with my finances."*

The better your financial decisions are, the better your financial picture will look. I know it sounds a little cheesy, but I don't know how to say it any other way. Good behavior produces good results!

Financial Freedom

So many of us come from homes with families that did not understand or prioritize good financial wellbeing. Most of us know all too well what it's like to have just enough. This experience shaped and molded our way of thinking about our finances. We began to believe that we would never be financially free nor be good stewards of our money. We started living the "you only live once" motto. The results have been catastrophic, and we can see how this lack of financial knowledge affected many generations before us. If we don't change, it will negatively affect many generations after us.

> **Caring about your finances is the highest form of self-care. Taking care of your finances is like a great day at the spa.**
>
> *Tony Cash*

What I'm about to say next may be a bit confusing but hopefully once you think about it, you'll gain clarity. I have seen people with bad money behavior expect to get the same results of those that exhibit good money behavior, for example becoming rich, wealthy, and financially sound. Trust me when I say that's not going to happen. Behavior equals results. Only good can come from good, and bad can come from bad.

You may ask, *"Does a person's behavior define them?"* As we think of the definition of behavior, it's simply defined as 'the way an individual, person or group of people act at any given time.' In other words, although a person's behavior is not a full description of who they are in totality, at any specific moment it would be fair to assume that is who they are.

Plato said *"Human behavior flows from three main sources: desire, emotion, and knowledge."* I would tend to agree with him. I also believe that good money behavior must start with these same three attributes, however not in same the order that Plato presented them. For good money behavior, the order of these words would be knowledge, desire and emotion.

Let us not forget that this chapter is all about how we reached the place of imprisonment by our financial decisions. Let's begin to examine these sources, starting with knowledge. Can a person really be expected to act upon what they have no knowledge of? Knowledge includes facts, information, and skills acquired through experience or education, the theoretical or practical understanding of a subject. So, we can see that without knowledge, a person is doomed to fail in whatever they try to achieve. That is why many people today find themselves in financial prison. They simply lack the knowledge or training to know and understand finances.

Secondly, let's examine the desire to be financially free. There is a quote that says, *"when your desire to succeed surpasses your need for comfort, then change begins."* I believe desire is necessary to have financial freedom, including the desire to end the life of mediocrity and self-loathing and the desire to be your best financially. A person follows their desires until they are either fulfilled or found to be unworthy, but they will always follow their desire! A misdirected desire keeps us from having financial freedom. Our focus is not on the goal; our minds and thoughts are not in a place that allow us to be better financially. Instead, they become distractions in life that keep us from giving our financial future the attention it deserves. The result is financial imprisonment; not having the freedom to enjoy life and all it can give us.

Lastly, let's examine the concept of emotions. Emotions are a normal part of life, and we can't do anything about having them per se. However, we must remain focused on the goal of financial freedom regardless of what happens in our lives. Many people lack financial freedom partly because they are led by their emotions, which in turn can lead to emotional spending. Simply put, emotional spending occurs when individuals spend money based on feelings and not based on sound financial principles. For instance, if they feel good, they spend; if they feel bad, they spend. Their financial emotions are unbalanced. Emotional spending can be even more disastrous if someone struggles with feelings like depression or a lack of self-worth. While emotional spending may give an instant feeling of comfort, in the end it will be detrimental to financial well-being.

I'll share a personal story to demonstrate how I apply this principle to my own life. I worked for one of the largest banks in America and we would have offsite team meetings with all the leaders of the company. I would see other leaders drive up in very expensive cars. As a matter of fact, some of them were in

> **Early concern and attention to your finances will prevent worry and scrambling later.**
>
> *Tony Cash*

the early stages of their careers but if you looked at their cars versus the car I drove, you would probably assume they were in at a more senior level than I was. Despite this, I never lost focus of my financial goal which was to achieve financial freedom. Yes, I noticed their nice cars, and in some instances, I even congratulated them on the 'achievement.' However, I never lost focus of *my* financial goal and I can proudly say that I am reaping the benefits of my delayed gratification. I kept my financial emotions in balance. It's safe to assume that many of those nice cars were bought because it was tied to an emotion, perhaps of pride or ego, lack of self-worth and/or wanting to be part of the "it-crowd."

Trust me. There will always be distractions and temptations that try to pull your financial focus out of focus. Stay strong, remain committed and keep your eyes straight ahead. My 'secret sauce' for staying focused on my financial goal is using the *"look but don't touch"* theory. This means that while I accept what others have acquired looks nice and I'm happy for them, it doesn't mean what they have is *for me*. I have learned that you never know what someone has sacrificed to acquire the things they have. I understood that my goal was to be financially free and that it was possible for me to achieve; the other leaders had different dreams that were more important to them. I didn't judge them, because everyone does not share the same financial goals and dreams that I did. My advice for you is to stay focused on your own financial goals and leave other people's business for them to manage.

Remember, to have good money habits and become wealthy, your financial emotions must be in balance. Healthy financial emotions equal financial freedom.

Take ACTION

What is causing me to emotionally spend?

How do I get my emotions under control, which in turn gets my spending under control, so that I CAN be financially free?

Our financial past isn't our financial path.

The mistakes we made yesterday are no longer the breadcrumbs in our financial lives.

We are living and behaving towards a better financial future; one where crumbs are not enough, we can have the whole loaf of the financial bread.

Tony

CHAPTER
3

The Path to Financial Freedom

Just like in life, there are so many paths we can take with finances. Some paths are good, and some paths are bad, but it's still each and every person's choice to take the path they want in life.

Today is decision day for your financial life.

As you read this book, you are now obligated to decide what you will do about your financial life.

- Will you reject poverty thinking?

- Will you change your negative financial decision making?

- Will you become more educated and learn about finances or will you say, *"I am comfortable being poor minded living paycheck to paycheck?"*

- Will you say, *"I enjoy not having everything I want and it's ok that I do not leave a legacy for my children's children?"*

Sometimes it's the smallest decisions in life that can change your life in the biggest way.

Tony Cash

Let's revisit the beginning of this book to remember how it started. I said, *"you are the key and it is all about you!"* Once you decide that you want financial freedom then that is the life you will have.

> **I'd like to live as a poor man with lots of money.**
>
> *Pablo Picasso*

You know, paths are interesting because for every path that starts, there is an end. To avoid danger when you walk on a particular path, it's especially important to have some idea of where the path is leading you. Paths are not meant for us to simply find them and just start walking; they are leading us somewhere that will ultimately end. We must be deliberate about where that path is leading us and the effect that walking that path will have on us. The financial path is no different; we must ensure that whatever financial path we choose is one that will have a positive outcome on our lives.

Our Relationship with Money

The way you saw money handled when you were a child is vital to your psyche, as it directly relates to how you handle your money today. We have all passed down what I call a **"Money DNA."**

Money DNA

The money behaviors you saw in your parent(s) or guardian(s) that have been physically and spiritually hardwired into you. Just like behavioral DNA, you could find it difficult to not repeat the very things you hated seeing your parents do with their money.

Building a positive relationship with money is vital. The way you see money and feel about money can be the difference between a successful, happy life and a miserable one. One of the most important things we can do regarding our relationship with money is to be careful of how we speak about it. It's extremely hard to love something you speak about in a negative way. Begin to picture yourself with money in a positive way. See yourself not only helping yourself with money but helping the next generation and changing the world. I have often thought about what I would do if I had more money. I realized that if I'm not doing something positive for the community or my fellow man with the small amount I have now, what makes me think a larger amount of money in my hand will change my character?

The way you think about money is connected to finding the right path to having more money. No one can ever start down the road to better finances with a negative view of money. Your thoughts, your emotions, your view, and your feelings about money must remain positive even when things are not going as well as you would like.

Stay the course and stay on a positive path. Make good decisions and don't allow anyone or anything to get you off the right path and lead you to negative thinking, poor money management and being financially imprisoned.

As I said before, just like in life there are so many paths we can take with finances. Some paths are good, and some paths are bad, but it is still each person's choice to take the path they want in life. Life will test us to see where we are in our relationship with money and whether we can handle more. As soon as we think we are on the right path, things will begin to happen to try and distract us. It is important that we are resolute in letting nothing get us off the path to financial freedom.

For example, one of the greatest distractions we can have is the immaturity of youth. When we are young, we are lulled into a false sense of believing that we have a lot of time before we must be concerned about the path we're on as it pertains to money. This could not be any further from the truth than the sun is from the earth! God gives us this youthful stage so that in our mature stage in life, we are positively prepared. God desires to bless us with what we need and want in life, but we must make sure that the path we choose is the one that leads to prosperity and not poverty.

Life is wonderful, and when we have money and good money habits within this life it becomes even more amazing.

Take the path to positive money management. Take the path to delayed gratification over impulsive spending and then you'll see this amazing thing called life flourish. Guess who will be the benefactor of all that amazing experience? You will! When God brings all that money into your life, be careful not to take the wrong path and lose the blessing. You were meant to have financial peace and joy, and the path to achieve that starts with good money management.

An Attitude of Gratitude

When we are grateful just for life and the many blessings it has afforded us, our attitude about money is different. We don't simply see money as a means of arrogance and perching ourselves above others. We see how blessed we are to have money and the opportunity to have wealth, and thus we don't abuse it. Perhaps that's why so many people abuse money and cannot seem to find wealth and financial freedom. They are not grateful and humble in spirit, and this leads to pride and waste, which are two ways of ending up poor. Gratitude is the state of being appreciative for what we have and caring for it.

I read a story in the bible about a guy named Joseph. He had a dream of becoming powerful and wealthy one day. His dream got him in trouble with his family. They believed he was being arrogant, and they sold him out. Joseph was a slave, and he went to prison for being accused of something he didn't do. If you read this story, you'll never read about Joseph's attitude changing. No matter where you find Joseph in the story, you find that he still has the right attitude. He ends up successful, to the point that he was able to take care of his jealous family.

Our attitude determines a lot about our financial success. Having an attitude of gratitude keeps us grounded, allowing us to smell the roses along the way to our financial success story. Do not forget about the people who are in need and always look for an opportunity to be kind. When we have the attitude of gratitude, the universe opens doors for us that no man can close.

Your relationship with God and money in this life are so important. If you can maintain a balanced relationship between success and gratitude, you will be able to live in peace and comfort, and at the same time help a lot of people.

Take ACTION

Decide on the life you desire and walk in it.

Don't get distracted by things that don't
bring you a healthy return.

Remember the path you take in your
financial life is your own.

Only you can decide which way you will go;
the path of financial freedom or the path to
financial imprisonment.

If you're struggling to make good financial decisions,
find someone who is making good financial decisions
and make them your new friend.

Tony

CHAPTER

4

Proven Financial Principles

My wife, Eleshia is a lifelong learner. She constantly reminds me and the children of the importance of reading. She is a big fan of reading and learning principles on different topics and so am I. Principles give you a roadmap to follow and you can revisit this roadmap to guide you back to the right path if you lose your way. Principles are standards that are time-tested, proven ideas.

Here are 4 important principles that will help you begin to experience financial freedom.

Knowledge is power. Information is liberating. Education is the premise of progress, in every society.

Kofi Annan

Principle #1: Educate Yourself

If you want to experience financial freedom, you must be willing to sit down and learn about money. Once you have learned about money, you'll never fear being broke again because you'll know what it takes to be wealthy.

When we are an educated people, we are a powerful people and financial freedom gives us power over our lives!

Think about it this way. If we are living riotously and then pray for financial miracles, it's not going to work. God doesn't just give us wealth; He gives us the power, wisdom, knowledge, and management skills to handle our money properly.

So often people are wishing and praying for financial success that will only come through hard work. I'm not saying that God can't bless you with money supernaturally, but most of the time we are going to get it through diligence and hard work.

> **The ability to say no to present spending and wasting will give you the ability to say yes in the future to a fearless life full of achievement and joy.**
>
> *Tony Cash*

One of my wife's favorite phrases is "delayed gratification." Delayed gratification is simply having the discipline to wait to get what you want now, so that you get a better deal later.

Delayed gratification has been a golden principle for me. The day that I decided to wait to spend my money and not waste it on something I wanted at that moment, I began to believe that my future would be amazing and exciting. Whatever you do in life, don't forget that you can trust the idea of delayed gratification. Simply put off the debt and emotional spending that comes with wanting to have things immediately and you can have a great life. Think about it; I can have one apple today. However, if I'm willing to take the apple seed and plant it, I can have an apple tree in a few years. Take the apple tree and watch how your children's children flourish.

Truthfully, a little waiting won't hurt you. As a matter of fact, it may help you gain a little more patience. Who can't use that?

Principle #2: Give Your Finances The Attention They Deserve

Finances can deteriorate mental and physical health if left unchecked. Stress and finances are unavoidable parts of life, and you'd be hard-pressed to find someone who hasn't experienced money troubles at some point. I know that it's quite easy to find a hole and hide from the tough world of personal finances, but that's not good. I compare this feeling to knowing that you must have a tough conversation with someone, and you know that the response may not favorable. Unfortunately, you still must have that conversation because if you don't, the matter will never be resolved. Do not put off tomorrow what you need to do today because every day you don't give your finances the attention they need, you go deeper in that hole you dug. Face your financial challenges head on. Keep a positive attitude and don't give up or run away from your responsibility. I really believe that once you face your financial responsibility, you will see changes that will come through your willingness to work hard and follow through.

Some people live their lives fearing the worst and when it comes to finances, some people are just downright frightened! They look at their current situation and automatically believe that there is no way out of the financial prison they are in and simply "do the time." There is a better way to look at it. I believe we should say *"although my financial situation looks tough, I am even tougher. I am even bolder and braver. When I finish dealing with my finances, I will be the boss and my finances will bow down to me; not the other way around."*

My First Book

I still remember the first time I decided I was finally ready to start writing my first financial book. I recall being so excited and yet so afraid. I thought of all the years I'd worked in finance, but seemed to keep questioning myself with thoughts like *"what did I have to offer that every other financial author could not offer?"* I remember really struggling to write the book. It certainly wasn't

> **Both poverty and riches are the offspring of thought.**
>
> *Napoleon Hill*

because I lacked the experience or education; it was because I was allowing fear to slowly creep in and paralyze me. I spoke to my wife, and she said *"Cash, you have at least a hundred books in you. Think about the 15+ years you have helped people become better with their money."* I began to loosen fear's grip because she helped me realize that fear is for the unprepared. I was more than prepared to help people better their financial lives. As I began to write the book, the information began to flow; all my experience erupted from the pit of my heart, and it was beautiful to feel all that knowledge flowing through my mind onto paper. The point I want to get across is that sometimes fear is not as big as we make it and maybe we need someone else who believes in us to help us conquer our fears.

> **Don't fear failure so much that you refuse to try new things. The saddest summary of a life contains three descriptions: could have, might have, and should have.**
>
> *Louis E. Boone*

There are times when God places purpose and a vision on your heart that is seemingly bigger than your ability. That is when fear rears its ugly head and tries to stop you and keep you from reaching your goals. Your response must be an emphatic *"fear will not stop me!"* Give your finances the attention they deserve and do not be afraid of failure because financial failure is not who you are... you're a financial winner!

Walk in Your Abundance

If you live long enough, life is going to present a fearful moment. Our job is to resist the fear, walk away from negative thoughts and not give in to worry and anxiety. I know a little something about fear because as I write this, I have just resigned from a great paying job. I made up my mind that I would not walk in fear, even for money. I will live the abundant life without fear and concern about failure because I'm focused more on success than anything else.

Principle #3: Invest More Than You Save

It is so important to be prepared for anything life brings you, especially financial issues. Anything can happen that turns your world upside down. That is why saving is important, and investing is vital. The year 2021 was an interesting year because while the rich got richer, the poor still dealt with inflation at a 7% rate even with stimulus funds. In other words, it may be raining on the rich and the poor, but the rich are once again under nice umbrellas. Remember these principles:

- Your money needs to grow.

- Saving accounts protect your money but investing protects and grows your money.

- You must not only save your money, but you need a return on your money so that you can keep up with the inflation monster.

At the time of this writing, gas is at an all-time high. Food is at an all-time high and living life in general is costing more. If you don't have the right investments, you are really losing money. We are really behind the proverbial 8 ball. Look at life and what it costs to live and ask yourself, *"Can the dollars I currently have buy the same amount of services and goods as it did last year?"* If the answer is no, then it's time to invest a little bit more.

Saving is the Gateway to Investing

Many people want to invest without saving but that's not possible. When you save, it becomes the building block to having enough to invest. **Your first investment is saving**. Once you have enough saved, now you can begin to think about where you want to invest your money. Open a savings account and use it as investment money. Think about how much it's going to take before you can invest an amount that will have a real effect on your finances **and** give you a tangible return.

If you are diligent in saving, you'll notice a difference in your personal wealth. I have seen people who set a certain savings goal and then take a part-time job to reach that goal a little faster. Whatever it takes to reach your savings goal, make it happen. You will find that it becomes easier to invest and expect a return when you have a great savings plan.

If you want to live in financial freedom, having a savings plan is vitally important as a gateway to investments. You might not be able to have or do everything you want right now, but it will be exciting when the day comes that you can see your savings account start at $500, then grow to $1000 and start that journey of investing towards your financial freedom. Hey, it may only make you a 'thousand-aire' and not a millionaire for the moment. However, if you keep good financial habits, one day you just might become that millionaire you desire to be.

> **How many millionaires do you know who have become wealthy by investing in savings accounts? I rest my case.**
>
> *Robert G. Allen*

You know, everything is beautiful in its season and if you will save now, you can live in financial freedom later.

Principle #4: Imagine Your Financial Future

When you imagine your financial future, you form a mental image of where you would like to be financially in your future. Imagine the joys you would like to experience, the peace you would like to experience and the happiness you believe you deserve and can only achieve through a financially sound life. It costs nothing to imagine. No special requirements are needed, and every one of us has the power to imagine.

In my opinion, wealth starts with a fundamental belief that you deserve all you are willing to work for and imagine. *Some people haven't started the path to wealth because they have a limited imagination.* I honestly believe that as a man thinks, so his life becomes.

IMAGINE...

- Yourself out of debt, out of despair, out of worry.

- Your life with:
    - No car payments
    - No house payments
    - Ability to travel when you want to

- The number of people you could help

- All the passions you could achieve if you had the money to do it

Do you see yourself financially free?

Do you see yourself living your best financial life?

I see financial success coming to you in a big way!

Create a vision board with pictures of the life you desire. Take time imagining yourself traveling and living with those things you want as well as the joyful feeling those accomplishments would bring. The more you imagine, the more it becomes real.

Albert Einstein has a famous quote that says *"Imagination is everything. It is the preview to life's coming attraction."* This reminds me of the scripture, *"Faith is the substance of things hoped for, the evidence of things not seen."* When you imagine, God will go to work to ensure that you have everything you need to be successful, so don't stop imagining and don't stop dreaming. Don't save your dreams for the nighttime...dream during the daytime when you're awake and you're able to adjust your dreams higher. When we dream during the day, we are giving ourselves permission to believe in our future. Your financial future is waiting, so don't let it down. You have places to go, people to see and dreams to accomplish!

All these principles are vital to your financial success. Do not be afraid, don't be shy and never allow yourself to imagine anything but positivity for your life.

Take ACTION

Write down three things you dream of doing once you've acquired the money.

Keep that piece of paper in a purse or wallet and take those dreams with you wherever you go.

Read them aloud as often as you can.

Let this piece of paper serve as a reminder that every action you take is for the success of those dreams.

The day I realized that I was ultimately responsible for my financial success, my life changed. I wasn't allowed to blame the government, my job, my mother or father for whatever offenses they caused me.

I had to look in the mirror and say, "I have to make up for all of their flaws and mine if I ever want to be rich!"

Tony

CHAPTER
5

Daily Steps to Financial Freedom

In this chapter, I want to help you take the steps needed to get to a place of financial freedom. My hope is that you will take each step one at a time and apply it to your life. You may recognize some of these steps, and my hope is that hearing them again allows you to know that you can have financial freedom.

You can do this! You can have everything you have always imagined in your life.

Step 1: Know your financial knowledge.

It's always important to know how much knowledge you have about a topic before you dive into it.

If you are a doctor, that's a great career. If you are a lawyer, that's a great career. To become a doctor or a lawyer, it takes great work and commitment. Learning about money is equally as important. I believe everyone needs a financial advisor, even doctors and lawyers. Why? Because a financial advisor's expertise and training will help you understand your financial goals and help you in achieving them. He/she will identify the best plans for your needs and show you how to make your money grow. The average person does not have the time nor expertise to deal with the complexity of money. Financial advisors save you a lot of time, effort, and resources. They take away the pressure and worry from you by dealing with the complex details of money management. The true goal of a financial advisor is to put you on the path to financial freedom and keep you there.

It's important to have financial knowledge but all of it does not have to be in your head. Allow someone to help you become your best financial self.

Step 2: Embrace Delayed Gratification

Delayed gratification is the ability to resist the temptation of instant pleasure. Instead of giving in to temptation, you hold out in the hopes of getting a better or longer-lasting future reward.

Suppose you desire a new fancy car (or "whip" as the young people say it). When you think about it, you know that you have not yet taken the time to secure your financial future or retirement. Desiring a car is not a bad thing, because maybe you've worked hard and really feel you deserve to have that car. In this case, you should first ensure that your financial future is secure. Instead of having to pay a

> **The sign of maturity is the ability to accept delayed gratification.**
>
> *Peggy Cahn*

monthly note to get that car now, exercise delayed gratification and you will be able to buy that car without needing to finance the cost. The car is paid in full. You are not paying outrageous interest, and no one can ever take the car away from you because it's paid for. Sure, you had to wait for a while and perhaps the wait was painful but look at the how the benefits of delayed gratification fully outweigh being impulsive and in a hurry!

People with a true rich mindset care less about what you think about them and more about what they know about themselves. They know that if they delay the enjoyment of their money for a season that they will reap the benefits of their money for a lifetime.

Ask yourself, *"Am I so concerned with what people think about me that I am willing to throw away my financial future?"*

Set your long-term goal and give your full effort. I know it's easy to want to fit in with the crowd and be the big fish in a little pond. However, that is not the best use of your time and money. It's best used through trusting that the time and money God has given you is not meant to work against each other but collaboratively. When you allow yourself the pleasure of waiting on what you want now so that you'll get what you'll need in the future, you will be playing a winning hand! Trust me, waiting isn't so bad. As a matter of fact, if you can just trust the process, you'll see the beautiful fruit that grows from the small seed you planted through delayed gratification.

Step 3: Get your emotions under control.

First, let me say that I don't think it's wrong to have emotions. However, I do believe you should work on keeping your emotions under control when it comes to your finances. So many people don't understand that they are emotional spenders. They spend money when they are happy, when they're sad, when they're bored and when they want to impress others. In essence, these people use money like medicine for every emotional moment. The problem with that type of thinking is that it's causing them to be poor.

Let's look at what emotions are. Emotions start as feelings, until we express them with actions. Anger, for example, isn't a bad emotion until we allow anger to cause us to respond in a detrimental way. That's why understanding emotions are so vital. When we understand our emotions, we discover that it's not the emotions that have power. It's allowing emotions to affect us to action. To avoid financial despair caused by emotions, we must properly contain them. Do not allow your emotions to lead you to poor judgment and/or risky behavior.

When you become aware of what's going on inside of you, then you can start to take control of your emotions instead of letting them take control of you.

I am fully aware of what is happening inside of me and won't allow it to affect my world outside of me. You can only truly make an informed decision that will positively affect your life when you can master your emotions. Stand strong on your core values and beliefs.

The secret to getting control over your emotional spending, as it relates to financial decisions, is being aware of your triggers. Embrace the idea that if you can control your emotions, you can control your spending. Now, you can be in charge of your wealth!

Step 4: Surround yourself with financially sound people.

Surround yourself with financially sound people. I have seen money cause so many problems for people in their lives. I have known good people who don't realize that keeping company with people who mismanage their money can affect the way they manage their own money.

As a child, my mother used to remind me of how important it was that my friends were good people. Her words were "monkeys see, monkeys do!" When you find yourself adopting bad money habits you can probably find the root cause by looking in one or two places. The first place you want to look is obvious; within yourself. Accepting responsibility for your own behavior is the number one characteristic for success in any area. The second place is one of the most overlooked areas that affect our success in life; the company we keep.

History says that Mozart was a musical prodigy, and we celebrate his genius on many levels. However, there are some who think the world is full of Mozarts who don't have the same opportunity or the same environment to cultivate their gift. Mozart's father was a minor composer and a music teacher and having a music teacher in the house certainly gave Mozart an environment that allowed him to flourish in his gift. If his father had been a carpenter or in a profession other than music, would Mozart be the composer we know today? Maybe so, but maybe not. However, I would venture to say that the Mozart we know today was based on 50% genetics from his parents and being blessed by the fact that his father was a music teacher. The people within your environment affect you more than you know.

I would implore any of you who struggles with finances to take notice of the type of financial behavior exhibited by the people around you. Carefully examine how their behavior could be influencing your own thoughts about money. I believe it's hard to be dry in water. Whatever and whoever we are around and cultivate with the most, affects us and influences our thinking, behavior, and abilities. If you're struggling financially, find a class to take on finances and/or find a strong financial circle or network to become a part of. Whatever you do, don't go at it alone. You are better than that. I know it and so do you.

As you work to become a better thinker as it relates to your money, let's recap a few of the strategies mentioned previously and learn a few new ones that I know will help you:

Strategy #1: List all your goals and your vision for your financial life. It becomes easier to achieve what you believe when you put it on paper.

Strategy #2: Meditate on what life will look like once you are debt-free and living the financially free life. We all spend time in thought, so since we have to engage in thinking anyway, it may as well be full of beautiful debt-free ideas.

Strategy #3: Read more about how to handle money. I have family and friends who bought my book, but I know they have never read it. How do you get to an unknown destination without reading a map?

Strategy #4: Don't stress about money but do stress the importance of handling money the right way. Many times, we stress about money without placing that stress on learning the right behaviors so that we have money. Don't let the fear of not having money overtake you, but don't be so fearless that you lose a healthy fear of how you handle money.

Strategy #5: Be open about what you don't know about money. No one can help you if they aren't aware that you need help. Don't allow pride to deter you from asking for help with your finances. Even doctors, attorneys and clergy need help financially, but it seems like the clergy is the only one willing to ask. (You'll get that later).

Strategy #6: Incorporate giving to others in the financial plan for your life. I have found that blessings really do come to those who give with a cheerful heart. Find a person or an institution to share your wealth with. You will find it both a personal blessing and a spiritual one.

Strategy #7: Enjoy your wealth. I know how hard it is to stop and smell the roses sometimes once you're on your wealth-building journey. You can become so driven to have a better financial future that you forget to enjoy an ice cream or two right now. Learn to appreciate your sacrifice and as you do small little things along the way, you'll feel energized to keep saving and investing towards a brighter future.

Take ACTION

Write down all your debts from smallest to largest.

Mark each one off as you pay it off.

You are a winner in your finances,

and just because you have had a few blips on the radar screen it doesn't mean you are a loser.

It simply means that to win you have some hurdles to overcome but thank God you are a jumper!

Tony

CHAPTER

6

Your Journey Begins Now

I hope reading this book was a blessing to you. I hope that it encourages you and reminds you that you were created to be financially healthy. I have been so blessed to be able to dedicate my time to writing this book for you and I hope you enjoy it as much as I enjoyed the process. I honestly believe every word in this book and more than that, I have tried my best to live them daily. I know that you can live the abundant life; all you have to do is believe in yourself, trust in the process you've read in this book and never ever give up. All your dreams will come true.

> **Before you can become a millionaire, you must learn to think like one. You must learn how to motivate yourself to counter fear with courage.**
>
> **Thomas J. Stanley**

My hope is that as you are on this journey to financial wellbeing, that you will never doubt your ability to be wealthy. Never look at your current situation and assume there is not a better future for you, because there is.

Take ACTION

As you begin your path to financial freedom, pledge to yourself the following:

Today I am starting the journey to a better financial life. I accept that there were mistakes I made in my finances. I accept that there was knowledge that I did not have regarding my finances. I realize that my faith and resolve to be a better steward of my finances is the key to me having financial peace, financial joy and the life I have always dreamed of.

I pledge to myself to remain true to the idea of good financial behavior. I pledge to myself to live a financially free life.

You are not at the end of your financial rope; you're swinging towards an amazing financial landing place.
Don't let go and don't give up!'

Tony

CHAPTER

7

Life Principles on Finances

Financial Quotes

It's not how much money you make, but how much money you keep, how hard it works for you, and how many generations you keep it for.

Robert Kiyosaki

Wealth is the ability to fully experience life.

Henry David Thoreau

What we really want to do is what we are really meant to do. When we do what we are meant to do, money comes to us, doors open for us, we feel useful, and the work we do feels like play to us.

Julia Cameron

Many people take no care of their money till they come nearly to the end of it, and others do just the same with their time.

Johann Wolfgang von Goethe

You can only become truly accomplished at something you love. Don't make money your goal. Instead, pursue the things you love doing, and then do them so well that people can't take their eyes off you.

Maya Angelou

Enjoying Money

Before you speak, listen. Before you write, think. Before you spend, earn. Before you invest, investigate. Before you criticize, wait. Before you pray, forgive. Before you quit, try. Before you retire, save. Before you die, give.

William A. Ward

The person who doesn't know where his next dollar is coming from usually doesn't know where his last dollar went.

Unknown

Money does not buy you happiness, but lack of money certainly buys you misery.

Daniel Kahneman

Money Wisdom

That man is richest whose pleasures are cheapest.

Henry David Thoreau

Money is multiplied in practical value depending on the number of W's you control in your life: what you do, when you do it, where you do it, and with whom you do it.

Tim Ferriss

Great Money Thoughts

Rich people plan for four generations; poor people plan for Saturday night.

Gloria Steinem

Don't go broke trying to look rich; act your wage.

Quotes.com

When people ask what you did to become wealthy, answer them the opposite of what you did to become poor.

Tony Cash

Become so financially secure that you forget that its payday.

Money.com

Funny Money Quotes

There is no way I was just born to pay bills and die; I'm too smart, too bright and simply too cute for that.

Tony Cash

The quickest way to double your money is to fold it up and put it in your back pocket.

Will Rogers

Black Friday Special: stay at home and save 100 percent.

Tony Cash

"The Poor You Don't Have To Be" Quotes

Poor thinkers can make a whole lot of money; they just can't seem to make a whole lot of sense with their money.

Tony Cash

Poor thinkers are overly concerned about everything except what they should be concerned with. They are concerned with what people are doing, the latest fashion or entertainment. All their concerns give them useful useless information.

Tony Cash

Rich Ideas

Rich people don't hear well until you're talking about something that will bring them a return on investment... Meanwhile poor people are always just returning things they bought.

Tony Cash

Rich thinkers actually do get sick and tired, but the difference between them and poor thinkers is they actually do something about it.

Tony Cash

Giving Back

Remember that the happiest people are not those getting more, but those giving more.

H. Jackson Brown Jr.

At the end of the day it is not about what you have or even what you've accomplished... it's about who you've lifted up, who you've made better. It's about what you've given back."

Denzel Washington

Giving back is a magical feeling that the giver gives the receiver and the receiver can pass it on giving it to others.

Tony Cash

Giving isn't just about making a donation; it's about making a difference.

Kathy Calvin

Take ACTION

Knowledge is power, but applied knowledge
is the key to transformation.

Don't just read these principles; apply them
to your life as you work towards your
financial freedom!

You may know how much money you have,
but that doesn't mean you understand
*how much money you **can** have.*

Tony

About the Author

Tony Cash lives in Atlanta, Georgia with his wife, Eleshia, and their two children, Kennedy and Jackson. Tony believes that everything in life starts with understanding how important people are; without people, you have no one to affect or influence. He believes that every person should have at least one thing they would do if they weren't paid to do it. Thirdly, Tony believes that without purpose we may be alive, but we are not living! At the end of the day when we realize The Who, The What, and The Why to our lives we will have lived a life worth living!

Tony is the founding and senior pastor of Global Leadership Christian Center where his passion for people living out their purpose has taken a small group of people from a living room to a vibrant, committed congregation.

Tony's passionate teaching coupled with life-changing practical wisdom has impacted not only the church but the surrounding community also. He is also the author of *"Eye Know Why You're Broke; Do You?"* which is the first book he wrote to share his financial wisdom. Tony has worked as financial leader in one of the largest banks in America and some of the best wealth management companies. He holds a Bachelor of Science degree in Business Administration, and this coupled with his 20 years of financial experience has afforded him the opportunity to be a sought out financial advisor and coach to many people as well as hold regular life changing financial seminars. Tony Cash teaches a three-prong approach to life. The whole sum of the person includes both spiritual and financial health. Tony lives by the motto, *"I will not die without Christ, I will not die unhappy, and I will not die poor."* Every decision he makes revolves around these three things. These principles are what he shares with those around him.